TOSHIBA
Fly Emirates
MasterCard

Glory in Union

Pitch Publishing Ltd
9 Donnington Park
85 Birdham Road
Chichester
West Sussex
PO20 7AJ

Email: info@pitchpublishing.co.uk
Web: www.pitchpublishing.co.uk

First published by Pitch Publishing 2023

1

A CIP catalogue record for this book is available from the British Library.

13-digit ISBN: 9781801503808
Design and typesetting by Olner Pro Sport Media. Visit www.olnerpsm.co.uk
Printed in India by Thomson Press India Ltd

Glory in Union

The Rugby World Cup

Matthew Bazell

pitch

20 June 1987, Eden Park, Auckland
In the final, France's Serge Blanco and Philippe Sella tackle New Zealand's Sean Fitzpatrick.

1987
Australia and New Zealand

1987: New Zealand and Australia

126 **Top points scorer was New Zealand's Grant Fox**

In 1883 the Home Nations Championship was created, featuring England, Scotland, Wales and Ireland; when France joined the tournament in 1910 it became the Five Nations. Rugby made its debut as a summer Olympic sport in 1900 when France won the gold medal, although the 1924 Games in Paris would be the last time that it was an Olympic sport (excluding the sevens). In 1930 FIFA created football's inaugural World Cup which would over the decades become the biggest sporting tournament on the planet. Despite FIFA's success, it failed to inspire rugby and also cricket to also follow suit. There were global tournaments and no clear and defining competitions to declare who the world champions of those sports were. It would not be until 1985 when a proposal was accepted by the International Rugby Football Board (IRFB) to stage a World Cup and the vote was won by 10-6. Australia, New Zealand and France were unanimously in favour of a world tournament, with the boards from England and Wales split. Scotland and Ireland both voted against, but once the tournament happened in 1987 they decided they didn't want to be left out. One of the countries that voted in favour was South Africa; however, the Springboks would not get the chance to participate in the first two World Cups due to the apartheid regime, which resulted in their isolation from the international stage in both sport and entertainment. In the years to come the South Africans would be allowed back, and to date they have the best win ratio in the history of the tournament with an average of 3.20 points a game (New Zealand come second with 3.13).

There was no qualifying process for 1987. New Zealand, Australia, France, England, Ireland, Scotland and Wales were part of the IRFB board and therefore were automatically in. The rest of the participants were by IRFB invite and this included the USSR, although they declined due to South Africa being a member of the IRFB, even though they weren't in the tournament. The first World Cup would set a precedent for every other one to follow, with the exception of 2003 – glory for southern hemisphere rugby. New Zealand versus Italy on 22 May 1987 was the first World Cup game and the All Blacks destroyed the *Azzurri* 70-6 which at the time was a record international tally of points. The prestige of the tournament – it's fair to say – had not been set, as the game was played at midday on a Friday to a stadium that was half empty. New Zealand won heavily in the other two group games against Argentina and Fiji, then walked over Scotland in the quarter-finals. This set up a semi-final against a Welsh side who had eliminated England 16-3, but the All Blacks crushed the last home nation standing 49-6.

6 **Craig Green and John Kirwan, both of New Zealand were the tournaments' leading try scorers with six each**

The day previously, Australia had been fully expecting to beat France in the other semi-final at the Sydney Concord Oval. The co-hosts were the pre-tournament favourites and went ahead on three separate occasions. Fly-half Michael Lynagh would miss crucial kicks to extend the lead, allowing France to come back and win 30-24, with a dramatic try from Serge Blanco in the dying moments settling a classic encounter. Australia would lose in the bronze medal match to Wales in what stands today as the best ever World Cup performance by the Dragons. Once again the Wallabies were beaten by a converted try in the last minute in a dramatic encounter. An Adrian Hadley try in the far corner had given Wales a chance to win the game with a conversion, albeit from a wide angle, and when Paul Thorburn kicked the ball through the posts, the pitch was invaded by hundreds of delighted Welsh fans, even though there were still a few seconds left on the clock!

1987 goes down as the World Cup that was won with very little drama, including the final, as a lacklustre France couldn't produce the heroics that they had managed in the semi-final. New Zealand were the strongest team in the tournament and won every game at a canter. In front of 48,035 home fans at Eden Park they comfortably beat the French 29-9, and for the first time a team were now able to proclaim themselves the world champions of rugby.

Pool 1

Australia	19	6	England
Japan	18	21	USA
England	60	7	Japan
Australia	47	12	USA
England	34	6	USA
Australia	42	23	Japan

	P	W	D	L	PF	PA	Pts
Australia	3	3	0	0	108	41	6
England	3	2	0	1	100	32	4
USA	3	1	0	2	39	99	2
Japan	3	0	0	3	48	123	0

Pool 2

Canada	37	4	Tonga
Ireland	6	13	Wales
Tonga	16	29	Wales
Canada	19	46	Ireland
Canada	9	40	Wales
Ireland	32	9	Tonga

	P	W	D	L	PF	PA	Pts
Wales	3	3	0	0	82	31	6
Ireland	3	2	0	1	84	41	4
Canada	3	1	0	2	65	90	2
Tonga	3	0	0	3	29	98	0

Pool 3

New Zealand	70	6	Italy
Argentina	9	28	Fiji
New Zealand	74	13	Fiji
Argentina	25	16	Italy
Fiji	15	18	Italy
New Zealand	46	15	Argentina

	P	W	D	L	PF	PA	Pts
New Zealand	3	3	0	0	190	34	6
Fiji	3	1	0	2	56	101	2
Italy	3	1	0	2	40	110	2
Argentina	3	1	0	2	49	90	2

Pool 4

Romania	21	20	Zimbabwe
France	20	20	Scotland
France	55	12	Romania
Scotland	60	21	Zimbabwe
Romania	28	55	Scotland
France	70	12	Zimbabwe

	P	W	D	L	PF	PA	Pts
France	3	2	1	0	145	44	5
Scotland	3	2	1	0	135	69	5
Romania	3	1	0	2	61	130	2
Zimbabwe	3	0	0	3	53	151	0

Quarter-Finals

New Zealand	30	3	Scotland
Australia	33	15	Ireland
Fiji	16	31	**France**
England	3	16	**Wales**

Semi-Finals

Australia	24	30	**France**
New Zealand	49	6	Wales

Third place play-off

Australia	21	22	**Wales**

Final

New Zealand	29	9	France

25 May 1987, Athletic Park, Wellington
In Pool 2, Ireland's Michael Bradley kicks the ball away against Wales. The Dragons won the game 13-6.

3 June 1987, Concord Oval, Sydney
Hosts Australia take on Japan in Pool 1 and beat the 'Cherry Blossoms' 42-23.

29 May 1987, Showgrounds Oval, Palmerston North
Tonga players perform the Sipi Tau before their Pool 2 clash with Wales.

New Zealand's
Finest Be

7 June 1987, Concord Oval, Sydney
Ireland take on Australia for a place in the semi-final. The Wallabies came out on top 33-15.

29 May 1987, Showgrounds Oval, Palmerston North
Tonga's Talai Fifita makes a pass in a Pool 2 clash versus a green-shirted Wales.

22 May 1987, Eden Park, Auckland
Action from the first ever World Cup game, as hosts New Zealand take on Italy. Here Craig Green is surrounded by Italian players.

14

23 May 1987, Lancaster Park, Christchurch
Scotland's Roy Laidlaw makes a pass during a Pool 4 tie with France. The game ended 20-20 and there would not be a tied game in the World Cup for another 20 years, when in 2007 the score ended 12-12 between Japan and Canada.

8 June 1987, Ballymore, Brisbane
England's Richard Harding runs with the ball in a quarter-final tie against Wales. The Welsh won 16-3 and would be the last home nation standing going into the quarter-finals.

XERO

13 June 1987, Concord Oval, Sydney
Philippe Sella of France runs through the Australian defence to score a try in the semi-final, in which Les Bleus won 30-24 to advance to the final.

TSU

14 June 1987, Ballymore, Brisbane
New Zealand players perform the Haka before the semi-final against Wales.

20 June 1987, Rotorua International Stadium, Rotorua
Wales's Paul Thorburn is about to pass to Adrian Hadley (right) who will score the try that set up a famous Welsh victory in the bronze medal match.

20 June 1987, Eden Park, Auckland
In the final, New Zealand's John Kirwan evades France's Philippe Sella to score a try in a 29-9 victory.

20 June 1987, Eden Park, Auckland
David Kirk lifts up the Webb Ellis Cup, as New Zealand becomes the first ever nation to be able to call themselves world champions.

NEW ZEALAND
ALL BLACKS

1991
England, Scotland, Wales, Ireland and France

19 October 1991, Murrayfield, Edinburgh
Western Samoa's Sila Vaifale charges through the Scottish defence in the quarter-final.

1991: England, Scotland, Wales, Ireland and France

68 **Top points scorer was Ireland's Ralph Keyes**

If the first World Cup took place in the country that is considered the best rugby-playing nation, the second tournament brought the game back home to its very origins. Just like in football, the first international match in rugby was when England met Scotland in 1871, the Scots winning in front of 4,000 fans (in football this match occurred in Glasgow a year later in 1872 when a 0-0 draw was played out to, once again, a crowd of 4,000). Some 120 years after that first match the two sides met in the semi-final of the World Cup, England edging a low-scoring affair 9-6. The game is best remembered for Gavin Hastings missing a close-range penalty while the scores were tied, to which he insists today with a smile, '[It] is not an iconic moment!' Before the kick the commentator remarked, 'There's nobody on the England side that believes he'll miss this one.' However, the kick was sliced and the ball went wide of the right-hand post. Hastings would later say, 'If I could erase that from my memory bank, erase that from history, I would do so. That's life, I'm glad it was me that missed it instead of one of my team-mates because I could handle it. I went on to captain the Lions; I went on to score more points playing in World Cups for Scotland. Pisses me off though!'

England, France, Ireland, Scotland and Wales were all joint hosts with 19 different grounds chosen as venues across the five nations. With apartheid South Africa still isolated and sanctioned from the international community, the only African representatives in the tournament were Zimbabwe, who would be competing in their second, and to date, last Rugby World Cup. Of the overall 16 nations competing, half did not have to go through a qualifying process as they had reached the quarter-final stage in 1987. Western Samoa were the only team making their tournament debut and would cause a major upset by beating Wales 16-13 at Cardiff Arms Park. The Welsh, who had been semi-finalists in 1987, were knocked out in the group stage despite playing three games on home soil.

6 **David Campese of Australia and Jean-Baptiste Lafond of France were the tournaments' leading try scorers with six each**

Before beating Scotland at Murrayfield, England had to overcome France in Paris, in a quarter-final considered today one of the most violent and brutal games in the history of the sport. Awaiting in the final were an Australian side spearheaded by the opinionated and charismatic David Campese. The Wallabies had faced a massive scare against Ireland in the quarter-final in Dublin and were trailing 18-15 in the closing moments after a try from Gordon Hamilton. Australia had the option to take a penalty which would have levelled the game, but instead went for the win and the gamble paid off with Michael Lynagh scoring a try with just three minutes to go as a raucous Lansdowne Road suddenly fell into silence. This set up a semi-final with the defending champions New Zealand in which tries from Campese and Tim Horan defeated the All Blacks.

In the build-up to the final, Campese had been critical of England's tough and aggressive style of play, used to wear teams down, which had served them well since losing to New Zealand in the opening group game. Senior members of the England team including Rob Andrew and captain Will Carling were said to have made the decision to play a more open and expansive game, but the change of style didn't give the players enough time to adapt. Despite having most of the possession, England went into the break 9-0 down thanks to a Lynagh penalty and a try from Tony Daly which would be the only one of the game. In 1991, Twickenham still had open sections of standing and wasn't all-seater like it is today. The crowd were certainly more animated and vocal than what you would expect from today's typical sporting crowd, especially ones who were lucky enough to obtain tickets for a World Cup Final. As England pushed forward at the end, with the score at 12-6 the home crowd were roaring them on in a fevered manner, but the Aussies held on and a pitch invasion followed. For the second World Cup Final in a row, Oceania had beaten Europe.

World Cup debutants: **Western Samoa**

Pool 1

England	12	18	New Zealand
Italy	30	9	USA
New Zealand	46	6	USA
England	36	6	Italy
England	37	9	USA
Italy	21	31	New Zealand

	P	W	D	L	PF	PA	Pts
New Zealand	3	3	0	0	95	39	6
England	3	2	0	1	85	33	4
Italy	3	1	0	2	57	76	2
USA	3	0	0	3	24	113	0

Pool 2

Scotland	47	9	Japan
Ireland	55	11	Zimbabwe
Ireland	32	16	Japan
Scotland	51	12	Zimbabwe
Scotland	24	15	Ireland
Japan	52	8	Zimbabwe

	P	W	D	L	PF	PA	Pts
Scotland	3	3	0	0	122	36	6
Ireland	3	2	0	1	102	51	4
Japan	3	1	0	2	77	87	2
Zimbabwe	3	0	0	3	31	158	0

Pool 3

Argentina	19	32	Australia
Wales	13	16	W Samoa
Australia	9	3	W Samoa
Wales	16	7	Argentina
Wales	3	38	Australia
Argentina	12	35	W Samoa

	P	W	D	L	PF	PA	Pts
Australia	3	3	0	0	79	25	6
W Samoa	3	2	0	1	54	34	4
Wales	3	1	0	2	32	61	2
Argentina	3	0	0	3	38	83	0

Pool 4

France	30	3	Romania
Canada	13	3	Fiji
France	33	9	Fiji
Canada	19	11	Romania
Fiji	15	17	Romania
France	19	13	Canada

	P	W	D	L	PF	PA	Pts
France	3	3	0	0	82	25	6
Canada	3	2	0	1	45	33	4
Romania	3	1	0	2	31	64	2
Fiji	3	0	0	3	27	63	0

Quarter-Finals

France	10	19	**England**
Scotland	28	6	W Samoa
Ireland	18	19	**Australia**
Canada	13	29	**New Zealand**

Semi-Finals

Scotland	6	9	**England**
Australia	16	6	New Zealand

Third place play-off

New Zealand	13	6	Scotland

Final

Australia	12	6	England

6 October 1991, Cardiff Arms Park
Western Samoa perform their version of the Haka, the Manu Siva Tau, in a Pool 3 game against Wales. Despite home advantage Wales lost 16-13 in a stunning upset.

10
12

6 October 1991
Zimbabwe, in hoop shirts, take on Ireland in Dublin. The home team won 55-11 and Zimbabwe have not played in a World Cup since.

13 October 1991, Welford Road, Leicester
The legendary Zinzan Brooke breaks through the Italian defence to score New Zealand's first try in a 31-21 victory in Pool 1.

5 October 1991, Cross Green, Otley
Italy take on the USA in Pool 1. Cross Green, home to Otley RUFC. This was the smallest ground used in the tournament and 7,500 people were in attendance.

WORLD CUP
OTLEY

12 October 1991, Cardiff Arms Park, Cardiff
The Princess of Wales meets the Australian team, who would beat Wales 38-3.

AUSTRALIA
WALLABIES
USTRALIA
WALLABIES
AUSTRALIA
WALLABIES

12 October 1991, Cardiff Arms Park, Cardiff
David Campese runs through the Welsh defence as Australia condemn Wales to elimination in the pool stages.

19 October 1991, Murrayfield, Edinburgh
Scotland's Finlay Calder battles past Western Samoa's Steve Bachop in the quarter-final.

20 October 1991, Lansdowne Road, Dublin
With just three minutes to go and Ireland leading, Australia's Michael Lynagh scores the winning try as his team progress to the semi-final.

Parc Des Princes, Paris
A brutal quarter-final tie plays out between England and France.

Parc Des Princes, Paris
England's Micky Skinner (6) and Brian Moore celebrate against France as England win 19-10 to progress to the semi-final.

26 October 1991, Murrayfield, Edinburgh
England and Scotland compete for a place in the final. England won a low-scoring game 9-6.

27 October 1991, Lansdowne Road, Dublin
David Campese runs in for the try, as Australia secure a place in the final and eliminate the defending champions New Zealand.

2 November 1991, Twickenham, England
The Australian team line up before the final against England.

FLY CATHAY PACIFIC

2 November 1991, Twickenham, England
England and Australia compete in the second ever World Cup Final. Australia went on to win 12-6.

1995
South Africa

24 June 1995, Ellis Park, Johannesburg
President Nelson Mandela greets the South African team, led by Francois Pienaar, before the World Cup Final against New Zealand.

1995: South Africa

1995 was the first Rugby World Cup to be exclusively held in one country – in the very same nation that had been isolated on the world stage for several decades due to apartheid. It's the most iconic World Cup to date – it also inspired a Hollywood movie – and a tournament in which the importance went far beyond sport. Previously the lines in the sand had been drawn; in South Africa, rugby was a white man's sport that carried no relevance to the majority black population. In the film *Invictus*, the opening scenes portrayed black South Africans supporting England in a game against the Springboks. The dilemma for black South Africans in 1995 was clear. Why would they want to support the very same people who they viewed as their oppressors not so long ago? It had only been a few years since freedom was won, and by supporting the Springboks they would be cheering on a team which would have included people who believed in the previous regime. Nelson Mandela, however, was adamant that the achievement of the Springboks would be the achievement of the entire nation.

112 **Top points scorer was Thierry Lacroix of France**

Despite home advantage, the final was pitted as David versus Goliath. In this case Goliath went by the name of 20-year-old Jonah Lomu who had taken apart England in the semi-final. When asked after the game how to stop Lomu, England captain Will Carling had replied, 'I'm hoping not to see him again myself! He's awesome, he was a freak. Sooner he goes away the better!' In later years Carling said that the team had studied tapes of Lomu before the game and made the mistake of treating him like a normal player.

In the quarter-final, England had defeated the defending champions Australia 25-22 courtesy of a Rob Andrew drop goal in the last play of the game. Any hopes England had of making their second final in a row were destroyed by Lomu who scored four tries, with the first and most iconic one being when he brushed aside two England players then clattered over full-back Mike Catt like a monster truck running over a Mini. Catt would later say, 'If a 15 [full-back] has to make a tackle, it means 14 other people have missed that tackle.'

Earlier in the tournament, New Zealand had taken Japan apart 145-17 in what stands today as the most points scored in a single World Cup match. A month earlier, Scotland's Gavin Hastings had set a points record in one game when he scored 44 points against the Ivory Coast. That record lasted just over a week, and in the victory over Japan, New Zealand's Simon Culhane scored 45 of the points in a record that still stands today. The other record set in that game was for the most amount of tries scored in a World Cup game, as Marc Ellis registered six for the All Blacks.

7 **Jonah Lomu and Mark Ellis, both of New Zealand, were top try scorers**

The final was a classic, despite having no tries; indeed, the game carries the unique stat of having just two scorers, one on each side. New Zealand's 12 points were all scored from the boot of Andrew Mehrtens and South Africa's 15 were all kicked by Joel Stransky. With the score 9-9 at full time it would become the first final to enter into extra time. Had the score stayed level after extra time, the team with the most tries would have been declared the winner. No tries were scored, which was in contrast to New Zealand's form before the final; they had outscored their previous opponents by a combined margin of 315-104, yet couldn't break a South African defence which had only given away 55 overall points throughout the tournament.

With no tries scored, a drawn match after 100 minutes would have been decided on disciplinary records. However, after exchanging penalties, Stransky kicked a drop goal with eight minutes of extra time remaining to make it 15-12 and the Springboks were world champions in their debut tournament; a point made by South Africa's president of rugby during the after-match banquet, who also claimed that the results of the first two World Cups should be null and void because of his nation's absence, much to the disgust of the New Zealand team who walked out of the dinner after having their 1987 World Cup win disrespected by an ungracious host.

Ultimately, 1995 will be remembered positively, for Nelson Mandela in a team jersey and baseball cap, standing next to Francois Pienaar and celebrating the Webb Ellis Cup being lifted in the air.

Pool A

South Africa	27	18	Australia
Canada	34	3	Romania
South Africa	21	8	Romania
Australia	27	11	Canada
Australia	42	3	Romania
South Africa	20	0	Canada

	P	W	D	L	PF	PA	Pts
South Africa	3	3	0	0	68	26	9
Australia	3	2	0	1	87	41	7
Canada	3	1	0	2	45	50	5
Romania	3	0	0	3	14	97	3

Pool B

Italy	18	42	Western Samoa
Argentina	18	24	England
Western Samoa	32	26	Argentina
England	27	20	Italy
Argentina	25	31	Italy
England	44	22	Western Samoa

	P	W	D	L	PF	PA	Pts
England	3	3	0	0	95	60	9
W Samoa	3	2	0	1	96	88	7
Italy	3	1	0	2	69	94	5
Argentina	3	0	0	3	69	87	3

Pool C

Japan	10	57	Wales
Ireland	19	43	New Zealand
Ireland	50	28	Japan
New Zealand	34	9	Wales
Japan	17	145	New Zealand
Ireland	24	23	Wales

	P	W	D	L	PF	PA	Pts
New Zealand	3	3	0	0	222	45	9
Ireland	3	2	0	1	93	94	7
Wales	3	1	0	2	89	68	5
Japan	3	0	0	3	55	252	3

Pool D

Ivory Coast	0	89	Scotland
France	38	10	Tonga
France	54	18	Ivory Coast
Scotland	41	5	Tonga
Ivory Coast	11	29	Tonga
France	22	19	Scotland

	P	W	D	L	PF	PA	Pts
France	3	3	0	0	114	47	9
Scotland	3	2	0	1	149	27	4
Tonga	3	1	0	2	44	90	2
Ivory Coast	3	0	0	3	29	172	0

Quarter-Finals

France	36	12	Ireland
South Africa	42	14	Western Samoa
England	25	22	Australia
New Zealand	48	30	Scotland

Semi-Finals

South Africa	19	15	France
England	29	45	**New Zealand**

Third place play-off

France	19	9	England

Final

South Africa	15	12	New Zealand

25 May 1995, Newlands, Cape Town
South Africa take on defending champions Australia in Pool A. The hosts won the game 27-18 and would finish top of the group.

26 May 1995, Olympia Park, Rustenburg
Gavin Hastings scores one of his four tries against the Ivory Coast in Pool D. The 89-0 score still stands as Scotland's biggest victory in a World Cup.

3 June 1995, Pretoria
The Scotland team are dejected as France score in the final minute to seal a 22-19 victory.

CHESTER
THE
BESTE
TUKKIES
BOKKE
JAMES IS SMALL
BUT WE HAVE
BIG NAKA'S

10 June 1995, Ellis Park, Johannesburg
Boks supporters cheer their team to a 42-14 victory against Western Samoa.

11 June 1995, Loftus Versfeld Stadium, Pretoria
Scotland take on New Zealand in the quarter-final. The All Blacks, wearing white shirts, won the game 48-30.

10 June 1995, Kings Park Stadium, Durban
France take on Ireland for a place in the semi-final. Les Bleus came out on top 36-12.

VISA

11 June 1995, Newlands, Cape Town
Rob Andrew kicks a winning drop goal, as England get their revenge on Australia for the defeat in the final four years earlier.

17 June 1995, Kings Park Stadium, Durban
On a waterlogged pitch South Africa and France battle it out for a place in the final.

18 June 1995, Newlands, Cape Town
England take on New Zealand in the quarter-final.

18 June 1995, Newlands, Cape Town
Jonah Lomu unleashes havoc upon the English defence as the All Blacks beat England 45-29 to secure a place in the final.

GILBERT

24 June 1995, Ellis Park, Johannesburg
Joel Stransky kicks a drop goal in extra time that wins the World Cup for South Africa against New Zealand.

Heineke

24 June 1995, Ellis Park, Johannesburg
One of the most iconic moments in sports history. Nelson Mandela celebrates as South African captain Francois Pienaar lifts the Webb Ellis Cup.

1999

Wales, France, England, Scotland, Ireland and Northern Ireland

1 October 1999, Millennium Stadium, Cardiff
The regimental goats of the Royal Welsh Fusiliers and the Royal Regiment of Wales at the opening ceremony.

1999: Wales, France, England, Scotland, Ireland and Northern Ireland

102 **Gonzalo Quesada of Argentina was the tournament's top points scorer**

Cardiff Arms Park had hosted matches in the 1991 World Cup, but by 1999 a new Welsh national stadium had been built, which some would argue was the best stadium in the United Kingdom. The Millennium Stadium (it had received state funding from the Millennium Commission) was built for the fourth Rugby World Cup and would be the second-largest stadium in the world to also have a fully retractable roof. The opening game and final were scheduled to be played in Cardiff, making Wales the primary host nation.

The three dominant forces of southern hemisphere rugby would dominate the quarter-finals. Defending champions South Africa beat England in Paris, Australia defeated Wales in Cardiff, and New Zealand saw off Scotland at Murrayfield. After three World Cups, there had still been no winner from the northern hemisphere, and the one hope left was for France who knocked out Argentina at Lansdowne Road, to progress to the semi-finals. They would face New Zealand at Twickenham in what would be one of the all-time classic matches. The French were 10-6 ahead after 21 minutes but then the All Blacks took control of the game and scored 18 unanswered points courtesy of two tries by Jonah Lomu. His first had similarities to the famous try he scored against England in the previous World Cup, and summed up why he would be considered by many to be the most colossal force to have ever played the game. Lomu picked up the ball around 30 yards from the try line. He brushed past two French defenders and charged towards the line. The big man was surrounded by six French defenders – and at this point a normal player would be looking for a pass to keep the momentum. Instead Lomu powered past the defence in one of the all-time great World Cup tries.

When Lomu scored a converted try early into the second half, after he ran past five French defenders, New Zealand had a 14-point lead and looked to be on the way to their third final. France's Raphaël Ibañez recalled, 'We trailed but we were still hopeful. I remember telling the guys I totally believed we could do it. We're close to doing something great.' France would then pull off one of the all-time great performances and scored 33 unanswered points as they took a 43-24 lead. With 15 minutes remaining there was no coming back and New Zealand's Josh Kronfeld said of their collapse, 'You're in a comfortable situation, and you come out and everything changes. They're getting closer, oh my goodness we gotta score, then all of a sudden it's gone.' France's final try looked something more akin to the football World Cup. New Zealand fumbled the ball deep into the opposition half and a French player kicked the ball downfield. Olivier Magne chased it all the way into the New Zealand half and kicked it all the way to the try line where Philippe Bernat-Salles grounded the ball to score France's fourth try of the game.

8 **New Zealand's Joma Lomu scored the most tries**

Twelve years after appearing in the first World Cup Final, France were back in the sport's ultimate showpiece, this time to face that other powerhouse of Oceanian rugby, Australia. The Aussies had beaten South Africa in the other semi-final, which was also played at Twickenham. With the score level at 18-18 after 80 minutes the game had to be settled in extra time, and in a match where every point came about through kicking Australia emerged 27-21 winners.

The final in Cardiff was competitive up to the 60-minute mark, when Christophe Lamaison scored his fourth penalty of the afternoon to take France to within six points of Australia. It would be Les Bleus' last points of the tournament. The Wallabies took total control and scored 17 points without reply, with Ben Tune scoring the game's first try in the 66th minute. Australia's win marked the first time a country had won two World Cups, and in the following tournament they would be defending their title on home soil and would be fancying their chances of a hat trick of wins.

World Cup debutants: **Namibia and Spain**

Pool A

Spain	15	27	Uruguay
Scotland	29	46	South Africa
Scotland	43	12	Uruguay
South Africa	47	3	Spain
South Africa	39	3	Uruguay
Scotland	48	0	Spain

	P	W	D	L	PF	PA	Pts
South Africa	3	3	0	0	132	35	9
Scotland	3	2	0	1	120	58	7
Uruguay	3	1	0	2	42	97	5
Spain	3	0	0	3	18	122	3

Pool B

England	67	7	Italy
New Zealand	45	9	Tonga
England	16	30	New Zealand
Italy	25	28	Tonga
New Zealand	101	3	Italy
England	101	10	Tonga

	P	W	D	L	PF	PA	Pts
New Zealand	3	3	0	0	176	28	9
England	3	2	0	1	184	47	7
Tonga	3	1	0	2	47	171	5
Italy	3	0	0	3	35	196	3

Pool C

Fiji	67	18	Namibia
France	33	20	Canada
France	47	13	Namibia
Fiji	38	22	Canada
Canada	72	11	Namibia
France	28	19	Fiji

	P	W	D	L	PF	PA	Pts
France	3	3	0	0	108	52	9
Fiji	3	2	0	1	124	68	7
Canada	3	1	0	2	114	82	5
Namibia	3	0	0	3	42	186	3

Pool D

Wales	23	18	Argentina
Samoa	43	9	Japan
Wales	64	15	Japan
Argentina	32	16	Samoa
Wales	31	38	Samoa
Argentina	33	12	Japan

	P	W	D	L	PF	PA	Pts
Wales	3	2	0	1	118	71	7
Samoa	3	2	0	1	97	72	7
Argentina	3	2	0	1	83	51	7
Japan	3	0	0	3	36	140	0

Pool E

Ireland	53	8	USA
Australia	57	9	Romania
USA	25	27	Romania
Ireland	3	23	Australia
Australia	55	19	USA
Ireland	44	14	Romania

	P	W	D	L	PF	PA	Pts
Australia	3	3	0	0	135	31	9
Ireland	3	2	0	1	100	45	7
Romania	3	1	0	2	50	126	5
USA	3	0	0	3	52	135	3

Quarter-final play-offs

England	45	24	Fiji
Scotland	35	20	Samoa
Argentina	28	24	Ireland

Quarter-Finals

Wales	9	24	Australia
South Africa	44	21	England
Scotland	18	30	New Zealand
Argentina	26	47	France

6 November 1999, Millennium Stadium, Cardiff
Australia becomes the first nation to win the World Cup for a second time.

Semi-Finals

Australia	27	21	South Africa
France	43	31	New Zealand

Third place play-off

New Zealand	18	22	South Africa

Final

Australia	35	12	France

6 November 1999, Millennium Stadium, Cardiff
In the final, Australia's Matthew Burke runs with the ball as France's Olivier Magne looks on.

16 October 1999, Murrayfield Stadium, Edinburgh
Spanish scrum half Aratz Gallastegui (centre) releases the ball from the scrum during their Pool A game v Scotland.

GILBERT

14 October 1999, Millennium Stadium, Cardiff
Samoa's Pat Lam is tackled in a Pool D tie against hosts Wales. They had beaten the Welsh in Cardiff in the 1991 World Cup, and history would repeat itself as the Samoans caused another upset in 1999 in a 38-31 win. Wales, however, would top the group.

1 October 1999, Stade de la Mediterranee, Beziers
Fiji perform the Cibi before their Pool C tie with Namibia. They would beat the Africans 67-18 and finish second in the group and progress to the quarter-final play-off.

10 October 1999, Lansdowne Road, Dublin
Australia's Tim Horan runs away from the Irish defence in a Pool E tie in which the Wallabies came away as 23-3 winners.

2 October 1999, Twickenham, London
England's Martin Johnson wins the ball in a line-out against Italy, in a Pool B tie in which England won 67-7.

15 October 1999, Twickenham, London
England's Richard Hill lies injured in a Pool B game against Tonga.
England won 101-10 in one of the biggest points totals in World Cup history.

20 October 1999, Stade Felix Bollaert, Lens
Devastation for Ireland as they crash out to Argentina in the quarter-final play-off.

14 October 1999, McAlpine Stadium, Huddersfield
Jonah Lomu is a handful for the Italian defence as New Zealand take apart the Azzurri 101-3 in a Pool B tie. Ten New Zealand players scored tries during this game, with Lomu getting two.

24 October 1999, Murrayfield Stadium, Edinburgh
New Zealand's Norm Maxwell breaks through the Scottish defence in the quarter-final, in which the All Blacks won 30-18.

23 October 1999, Millennium Stadium, Cardiff
In a downpour in Cardiff Wales's Colin Charvis beats Tim Horan to the ball. Australia, however, would win 24-9 and progress to the semi-final.

24 October 1999, Stade de France, Paris
Johnny Wilkinson and Phil Greening fail to stop a drop goal from South Africa's Jannie de Beer as England crash out in the quarter-final.

31 October 1999, Twickenham, London
An epic semi-final tie between France and New Zealand. Olivier Magne salutes the crowd in victory as France come from behind to win 43-31 and progress to the final.

6 November 1999, Millennium Stadium, Cardiff
French winger Christophe Dominici is tackled by Australia's George Gregan and Stephen Larkham in the Rugby World Cup Final.

22 November 2003, Stadium Australia, Sydney
Jonny Wilkinson kicks the winning drop goal in the dying seconds against Australia in the final.

2003
Australia

2003: Australia

113 **Top points scorer was England's Jonny Wilkinson**

As in the inaugural tournament in 1987, the World Cup of 2003 was supposed have been co-hosted by both New Zealand and Australia. However, New Zealand's rugby board had a contract dispute with the organisers about signage rights in the stadiums, and so a decision was made that Australia would be the sole host. Eleven stadiums would host a combined number of 48 matches, with Georgia being the one country who were competing in their first World Cup.

The structure of the previous World Cup in 1999 would be viewed as too complicated as only the teams who finished top in each of the five pools were guaranteed a place in the quarter-finals. The other three positions would be decided in play-off games where the teams who finished second would play a team who finished third. In 2003, the group structure would be changed in favour of four pools of five teams, with the top two in each one progressing. For the first time at the World Cup, a bonus point system was introduced. If a team were to score four tries or more in a group game, or lose by no more than a seven-point margin, then they would get one additional point. The reward for any win also went up from three points to four, and has stayed that way to the present day.

There were some heavy beatdowns in the group stages by the strong teams upon the weaker ones. England's 111-13 defeat of Uruguay in Pool C is the fourth-highest points total in World Cup history, while Australia's 142-0 crushing of Namibia remains the biggest winning margin of all time. As usual, New Zealand were in a free-scoring mode; to date they have scored 1,023 points in the group stages over nine World Cups, 282 of which came in 2003, where in Pool D they crushed everyone in sight, with their 53-37 win over a spirited Wales being the lowest tally they scored over the four group games.

2003 had already been a great year for England, having won a grand slam in the Six Nations. They would go into the World Cup as favourites, and made a statement win in Pool C with a 25-6 defeat of South Africa. After seeing off Wales and France in the knockout rounds they would face the hosts in the ultimate chance to avenge the 1991 World Cup Final, where Australia had beaten England at Twickenham. The Wallabies had overcome the challenge of New Zealand in the semi-final, with the home crowd booing and singing over the haka ritual before kick-off.

For the final in the 83,000 capacity Stadium Australia in Sydney, the hosts got a perfect start after a kick to the corner by Stephen Larkham was caught by Lote Tuqiri for a try in the sixth minute. One England player would become synonymous with the 2003 World Cup, and his kicking skills became celebrated more than any of the nation's footballers. Jonny Wilkinson was the sole points scorer in England's 24-7 semi-final win against France and had also scored 23 of the points in the 28-17 win against Wales in the quarter-final. Against Australia in the final he added three first-half penalties to take England into a 9-5 lead, meaning that 56 of the team's last 61 points had come from the boot of Wilkinson. Before anyone could accuse England of being a one-trick pony, Jason Robinson scored a try to increase the lead to 14-5, and incredibly Wilkinson missed the conversion, albeit from a wide angle.

7 **Doug Howlett and Mils Muliaina, both of New Zealnd were top try scorers**

Australia fought back in the second half with three Elton Flatley penalties, the last of which was in the 81st minute. England led 17-14 deep into the second half of extra time but once again Flatley equalised via a penalty in the dying moments. There was still just enough time, however, for England to work the ball into Australian territory, and get it into the hands of Wilkinson who scored the most celebrated drop goal in English rugby history. 'There's no one you'd want more in that position than Wilko,' said captain Martin Johnson. Wilkinson's 113 points in 2003 still stands today as the second-highest individual tally of a single tournament and would contribute to his overall World Cup total of 277 points, making him the top points scorer in the competition's history. For the first time since 1966 England had won a sporting World Cup, and it remains the only one to date to have been achieved on foreign soil.

World Cup debutants: Georgia

Pool A

Australia	24	8	Argentina
Ireland	45	17	Romania
Argentina	67	14	Namibia
Australia	90	8	Romania
Ireland	64	7	Namibia
Argentina	50	3	Romania
Australia	142	0	Namibia
Argentina	15	16	Ireland
Namibia	7	37	Romania
Australia	17	16	Ireland

	P	W	D	L	PF	PA	Pts
Australia	4	4	0	0	273	32	18
Ireland	4	3	0	1	141	56	15
Argentina	4	2	0	2	140	57	11
Romania	4	1	0	3	65	192	5
Namibia	4	0	0	4	28	310	0

Pool B

France	61	18	Fiji
Scotland	32	11	Japan
Fiji	19	18	USA
France	51	29	Japan
Scotland	39	15	USA
Fiji	41	13	Japan
France	51	9	Scotland
Japan	26	39	USA
France	41	14	USA
Scotland	22	20	Fiji

	P	W	D	L	PF	PA	Pts
France	4	4	0	0	204	70	20
Scotland	4	3	0	1	102	97	14
Fiji	4	2	0	2	98	114	10
USA	4	1	0	3	86	125	6
Japan	4	0	0	4	79	163	0

Pool C

South Africa	72	6	Uruguay
England	84	6	Georgia
Samoa	60	13	Uruguay
South Africa	6	25	England
Georgia	9	46	Samoa
South Africa	46	19	Georgia
England	35	22	Samoa
Georgia	12	24	Uruguay
South Africa	60	10	Samoa
England	111	13	Uruguay

	P	W	D	L	PF	PA	Pts
England	4	4	0	0	255	47	19
South Africa	4	3	0	1	184	60	15
Samoa	4	2	0	2	138	117	10
Uruguay	4	1	0	3	56	255	4
Georgia	4	0	0	4	46	200	0

Pool D

New Zealand	70	7	Italy
Wales	41	10	Canada
Italy	36	12	Tonga
New Zealand	68	6	Canada
Wales	27	20	Tonga
Italy	19	14	Canada
New Zealand	91	7	Tonga
Italy	15	27	Wales
Canada	24	7	Tonga
New Zealand	53	37	Wales

	P	W	D	L	PF	PA	Pts
New Zealand	4	4	0	0	282	57	20
Wales	4	3	0	1	132	98	14
Italy	4	2	0	2	77	123	8
Canada	4	1	0	3	54	135	5
Tonga	4	0	0	4	46	178	1

Quarter-Finals

New Zealand	29	9	South Africa
Australia	33	16	Scotland
France	43	21	Ireland
England	28	17	Wales

22 November 2003, Stadium Australia, Sydney
Martin Johnson lifts the Webb Ellis Cup as England become the first northern hemisphere team to be crowned world champions.

Semi-Finals

New Zealand	10	22	**Australia**
France	7	24	**England**

Third place play-off

New Zealand	40	13	France

Final

Australia 17 20 **England**
(aet)

22 November 2003, Stadium Australia, Sydney
Jason Robinson scores a try to put England 14-5 ahead in the first half of the final against Australia.

15 October 2003, Suncorp Stadium, Brisbane
Fiji's Api Naevo throws a pass in their Pool B game v USA.

12 October 2003, Docklands Stadium, Melbourne
Canada's Winston Stanley passes from the ruck as Wales' Mike James looks on in the background.

19 October 2003, Subiaco Oval, Perth
Samoa's Terry Fanolua off-loads the ball in their Pool C clash with Georgia.

15 October 2003, Canberra Stadium, Canberra
The Tonga team perform their Sipi Tau before their Pool D match against Italy.

26 October 2003, Docklands Stadium, Melbourne
Samoa's players perform the Manu Siva Tau, before their Pool C tie against England.

8 November 2003, Docklands Stadium, Melbourne
South Africa and New Zealand face off in a scrum during their quarter-final tie. The All Blacks won 29-9.

9 November 2003,
Docklands Stadium, Melbourne
France's Jerome Thion receives treatment in his side's 43-21 quarter-final win against Ireland.

8 November 2003, Suncorp Stadium, Brisbane
Scotland take on Australia in the quarter-final. The hosts won by 33-16 to progress to the semi-final where they would face New Zealand.

16 November 2003, Stadium Australia, Sydney
Jonny Wilkinson looks on as England and France lock in for a scrum in the semi-final. England won 24-7 with all their points coming from the boot of Wilkinson.

15 November 2003, Stadium Australia, Sydney
Australia's Wendell Sailor takes on the New Zealand defence in the semi-final.

22 November 2003, Stadium Australia, Sydney
In the dying moments of regular time, Australia's Elton Flatley levels things at 14-14 and takes the final into extra time.

RUGBY WORLD CUP 2003
Australia
Engla
1 Tries
0 Conversions
2 Penalties
0 Drop Goals
11 Score
Second Half
UNISYS

22 November 2003, Stadium Australia, Sydney
Ben Cohen (far left), Matt Dawson (left) and Martin Johnson (right) offer encouragement to Jonny Wilkinson before he takes a penalty during the final against Australia.

RUGBY
2003
ILBERT

6 October 2007, Millennium Stadium, Cardiff
French players celebrate after a sensational win against New Zealand in the quarter-final.

2007
France, Wales and Scotland

2007: France, Wales and Scotland

105 **Percy Montgomery of South Africa was the tournament's top points scorer**

With the exception of four games in Cardiff and two in Edinburgh, the entirety of the tournament was played out across ten French cities. Ironically and surprisingly, France would end up playing in one of the Cardiff matches in the knockout rounds after finishing second in their group and losing home advantage. They would be beaten to top spot in Pool D by Argentina who would be one of the stories of the tournament. The South Americans had grown used to playing the hosts in the opening game; in 1999 they lost 23-18 to Wales and in 2003 they were beaten 24-8 by Australia. Instead of making it a hat-trick, Argentina handed France their first ever loss in the group stages, and their emergence saw Pool D justify its 'group of death' tag – given that Ireland were also in there.

The typical World Cup experience for the Irish is to make it to the quarter-final stage, and they go in to the 2023 tournament in France as one of the favourites to win it. In 2007, however, Ireland's 30-15 defeat to the Pumas of Argentina condemned them to their one and only elimination in the group stages. Argentina would go on to lose to South Africa in the semi-final, but would then beat France once again in the bronze medal match, in what still stands as their greatest performance in a World Cup.

Portuguese fans in the crowd waving the national flag and cheering would be something you'd associate with the other World Cup with the round ball. However, in 2007 Portugal were making their only appearance to date in the Rugby World Cup and there were cheers of delight from their fans when their team scored a try against New Zealand, despite being on the end of a 108-13 defeat in what goes down as the fourth-biggest win (by points total) in World Cup history.

Despite losing home advantage, France would put on their best performance of the tournament when they beat New Zealand in Cardiff. The All Blacks (wearing an unfamiliar grey kit) took a 13-0 lead and were looking to avenge the semi-final defeat they suffered to the French in 1999. Instead, lightning struck twice and *Les Bleus* once again came from a losing position to knock New Zealand out of the World Cup. This set up a semi-final in Paris against defending champions England in one of the most brutal and hard-hitting games in World Cup history. England were weaker than in 2003 but they still had the kicking skills of Jonny Wilkinson. They got the perfect start in the second minute when Josh Lewsey scored a try, but France responded by scoring three penalties in a row to take the lead. With just a little over two minutes to play England were 11-9 ahead, before Wilkinson scored a drop goal which the commentator described as 'déjà vu' from four years earlier. France could still win the game on a converted try, and desperately pressed the English defence in the dying moments, but England held firm and against all odds were back in the final.

8 **Bryan Habana of South Africa was the tournament's leading try scorer with six**

Such a scenario had looked impossible in the early stages of the tournament, not least after losing 36-0 in the group stages in what still stands as their record defeat in a World Cup, and their fifth heaviest defeat of all time. The team who inflicted that heavy loss upon England were waiting to dethrone them in the final. South Africa were heavy favourites but the game would be a tight affair dominated by kicking. The Springboks had won the 1995 final with kicking points only, and would do the same in 2007 against an England team who also found tries hard to come by against elite opposition. The flashpoint in the game would be the try that wasn't; with England trailing 9-3 early in the second half, Matthew Tait was tackled just before the goal line after an incredible forward run. The ball found its way to Mark Cueto on the wing and he scored what looked like a perfectly good try, but after a long video review, using multiple angles, it was judged that Cueto's left foot went out of play just before the ball was grounded. The margins for glory and despair down to inches. The game finished 15-6 and South Africa, instead of England, now had a repeat triumph, and were also becoming experts at winning World Cup Finals without scoring any tries.

World Cup debutants: **Portugal**

Pool A

England	28	10	USA
USA	15	25	Tonga
South Africa	36	0	England
Samoa	15	19	Tonga
England	44	22	Samoa
Samoa	25	21	USA
England	36	20	Tonga
South Africa	64	15	USA
South Africa	30	25	Tonga
Samoa	7	59	South Africa

	P	W	D	L	PF	PA	Pts
South Africa	4	4	0	0	189	47	19
England	4	3	0	1	108	88	14
Tonga	4	2	0	2	89	96	9
Samoa	4	1	0	3	69	143	5
USA	4	0	0	4	61	142	1

Pool B

Australia	91	3	Japan
Wales	42	17	Canada
Japan	31	35	Fiji
Wales	20	32	Australia
Fiji	29	16	Canada
Wales	72	18	Japan
Australia	55	12	Fiji
Canada	12	12	Japan
Australia	37	6	Canada
Wales	34	38	Fiji

	P	W	D	L	PF	PA	Pts
Australia	4	4	0	0	215	41	20
Fiji	4	3	0	1	114	136	15
Wales	4	2	0	2	168	105	12
Japan	4	0	1	3	64	210	3
Canada	4	0	1	3	51	120	2

Pool C

New Zealand	76	14	Italy
Scotland	56	10	Portugal
Italy	24	18	Romania
New Zealand	108	13	Portugal
Scotland	42	0	Romania
Italy	31	5	Portugal
Scotland	0	40	New Zealand
Romania	14	10	Portugal
New Zealand	85	8	Romania
Scotland	18	16	Italy

	P	W	D	L	PF	PA	Pts
New Zealand	4	4	0	0	309	35	20
Scotland	4	3	0	1	116	66	14
Italy	4	2	0	2	85	117	9
Romania	4	1	0	3	40	161	5
Portugal	4	0	0	4	38	209	1

Pool D

France	12	17	Argentina
Ireland	32	17	Namibia
Argentina	33	3	Georgia
Ireland	14	10	Georgia
France	87	10	Namibia
France	25	3	Ireland
Argentina	63	3	Namibia
Georgia	30	0	Namibia
France	64	7	Georgia
Ireland	15	30	Argentina

	P	W	D	L	PF	PA	Pts
Argentina	4	4	0	0	143	33	18
France	4	3	0	1	188	37	15
Ireland	4	2	0	2	64	82	9
Georgia	4	1	0	3	50	111	5
Namibia	4	0	0	4	30	212	0

Quarter-Finals

Australia	10	12	England
New Zealand	18	20	France
South Africa	37	20	Fiji
Argentina	19	13	Scotland

20 October 2007, Stade de France, Paris
South Africa celebrate a second World Cup triumph after beating England 15-6 in the final.

Semi-Finals

England	14	9	France
South Africa	37	13	Argentina

Third place play-off

France	10	34	Argentina

Final

England	6	15	South Africa

20 October 2007, Stade de France, Paris
South Africa celebrate defeating England in the final

20 September 2007, Millennium Stadium, Cardiff
Wales' James Hook heads for the tryline in their Pool B fixture with Japan.

9 September 2007, Chaban Delmas Stadium, Bordeaux
Irish captain Brian O'Driscoll bursts through an opposition tackle during the Pool D match v Namibia.

15 September 2007, Stade de Gerland, Lyon
New Zealand take on World Cup debutants Portugal. The game ended 108-13 as the All Blacks recorded the fourth-biggest points total in World Cup history.

LYON
5
4
5
14
Emirates

6 October 2007, Millennium Stadium, Cardiff
France's Sebastien Chabal, in action against New Zealand in the quarter-final. Chabal gained the nickname l'Homme des Caverness from French rugby fans which translates into The Caveman!

6 October 2007, Stade Velodrome, Marseille
England's Andrew Sheridan and Australia's Matt Dunning lock horns in a quarter-final tie and rematch of the 2003 final.

6 October 2007, Stade Velodrome, Marseille
England take on Australia in the quarter-final. The defending champions England won 12-10 courtesy of four Jonny Wilkinson penalties.

20 October 2007, Stade de France, Paris
Argentina take on Scotland in the quarter-final. The South Americans won 19-13 and 2007 would be Argentina's best ever performance in a World Cup.

7 October 2007, Stade de France, Paris
Argentina's Gonzalo Longo and Scotland's Sean Lamont jump at the line-out.

Orange

7 October 2007, Stade Velodrome, Marseille
South Africa's Juan Smith wins a line-out during their 37-20 victory over Fiji in the IRB Rugby World Cup quarter-final match.

9 September 2007, Parc des Princes, Paris
Samoa's players perform the Manu Siva Tau before their Pool A tie against South Africa.

13 October 2007, Stade de France, Paris
Jonny Wilkinson kicks a penalty to put England in the lead in the semi-final against France. Despite being weaker than the team that won in 2003, England managed to reach the final.

ediorbis

14 October 2007, Stade de France, Paris
South Africa take on Argentina in the semi-final. The Springboks put an end to Argentina's great World Cup with a 37-13 win.

9 September 2007, Parc des Princes, Paris
Bryan Habana, the star man of 2007, celebrates his fourth try against Samoa in Pool A.

20 October 2007, Stade de France, Paris
South Africa lift up the Webb Ellis Cup to equal Australia's record of two World Cup wins.

RUGBY
2007
Final

24 September 2011, Eden Park, Auckland
New Zealand's Piri Weepu (standing) leads the Haka during the Pool A match at Eden Park against France.

2011
New Zealand

2011: New Zealand

62 **Morné Steyn of South Africa scored the most points**

New Zealand are perhaps to rugby what Brazil are to football, yet after six World Cups the All Blacks had only won the trophy on one occasion: the inaugural tournament in 1987, in which they were the hosts. In 2011 the World Cup was back in New Zealand and the only outcome acceptable for the rugby-obsessed nation was for the All Blacks to win it for a second time. Japan and South Africa also had bids to stage the tournament, which for the South Africans would have meant two World Cups in two years, following hosting the football finals in 2010.

Japan had been hoping to be the first Asian country to host the World Cup but would have to wait until 2019 for that honour. They were pitted in Pool A with New Zealand and would finish bottom with just two points. Predictably, New Zealand finished top of the group, winning all four games by scoring an eye-watering 240 points. Of their four matches, the lowest total New Zealand scored was their 37 points in a win against France, who would also qualify by finishing second in the group, despite being on the end of a 19-14 defeat against Tonga in one of the biggest shocks in World Cup history. Tonga were 13-9 ahead with just over 15 minutes on the clock, then Fabrice Estebanez gave away a penalty for a dangerous tackle and was sent to the sin bin. Two penalty conversions by Tonga soon followed to make it a two-possession game, and the French were finished. However, they would go on to score a consolation try in the dying seconds which would carry importance in qualifying to the later stages. Tonga's 25-20 defeat to Canada meant that both themselves and France had two wins and two defeats, but France would finish second and progress due to having three bonus points to Tonga's one.

Rugby's two oldest superpowers, England and Scotland, were pitted together in Pool B. The two teams met in the final group game, with England having already qualified, and the Scottish in desperate trouble after a 13-12 defeat to Argentina. England beat their old rivals and for the first time in their World Cup history, Scotland had failed to make it to the knockout rounds. Of the home nations, Wales fared the best and came agonisingly close to making it to their first World Cup Final. They faced England's quarter-final conquerors France in a low-scoring game decided by just the one point. Wales were in their first semi-final in 24 years after seeing off Ireland in the previous round. With Wales 3-0 ahead against France in the 18th minute, their captain Sam Warburton was given a straight red card for a 'tip tackle' on Vincent Clerc. One commentator referred to it at the time as one of the most controversial decisions of any World Cup, but he also pointed out the rules – that if you take a player off his feet and into the air, it's your responsibility to bring him down with care. Warburton had been one of the players of the tournament, Wales had played well throughout, and now the game was suddenly tipped in favour of the out-of-form French, who won 9-8.

6 **Chris Ashton of England and Vincent Clerc of France were the tournament's top try scorers**

The final of New Zealand vs France was a repeat of the inaugural World Cup in 1987, which was also played at Auckland's Eden Park. In the six games leading up to the final, New Zealand had outscored their opponents combined by score of 293-65. In contrast France's margins were far tighter and they had an overall record of 152-116, and had lost two of their six matches. New Zealand were overwhelming favourites, yet the match would be – and remains – the lowest-scoring final and would be won by the slimmest of margins.

Before kick-off, France's response to the Haka was memorable and showed that they were up for a fight. They lined up in the V formation of an arrow and moved in unison towards the All Blacks midway through the ritual. They would receive a fine of £2,500 by the IRB for crossing the halfway line during the Haka. New Zealand's 8-7 win may not have been in the swashbuckling manner in which they would have hoped, but all that mattered was that they could now join their southern hemisphere rivals Australia and South Africa as record holders with two overall World Cup triumphs.

Pool A

New Zealand	41	10	Tonga
France	47	21	Japan
Tonga	20	25	Canada
New Zealand	83	7	Japan
France	46	19	Canada
Tonga	31	18	Japan
New Zealand	37	17	France
Canada	23	23	Japan
France	14	19	Tonga
New Zealand	79	15	Canada

	P	W	D	L	PF	PA	Pts
New Zealand	4	4	0	0	240	49	20
France	4	2	0	2	124	96	11
Tonga	4	2	0	2	80	98	9
Canada	4	1	1	2	82	168	6
Japan	4	0	1	3	69	184	2

Pool B

Scotland	34	24	Romania
England	13	9	Argentina
Scotland	15	6	Georgia
Argentina	43	8	Romania
England	41	10	Georgia
England	67	3	Romania
Argentina	13	12	Scotland
Georgia	25	9	Romania
England	16	12	Scotland
Argentina	25	7	Georgia

	P	W	D	L	PF	PA	Pts
England	4	4	0	0	137	34	18
Argentina	4	3	0	1	90	40	14
Scotland	4	2	0	2	73	59	11
Georgia	4	1	0	3	48	90	4
Romania	4	0	0	4	44	169	0

Pool C

Australia	32	6	Italy
Ireland	22	10	USA
Russia	6	13	USA
Australia	6	15	Ireland
Italy	53	17	Russia
Australia	67	5	USA
Ireland	62	12	Russia
Italy	27	10	USA
Australia	68	22	Russia
Ireland	36	6	Italy

	P	W	D	L	PF	PA	Pts
Ireland	4	4	0	0	135	34	17
Australia	4	3	0	1	173	48	15
Italy	4	2	0	2	92	95	10
USA	4	1	0	3	38	122	4
Russia	4	0	0	4	57	196	1

Pool D

Fiji	49	25	Namibia
South Africa	17	16	Wales
Samoa	49	12	Namibia
South Africa	49	3	Fiji
Wales	17	10	Samoa
South Africa	87	0	Namibia
Fiji	7	27	Samoa
Wales	81	7	Namibia
South Africa	13	5	Samoa
Wales	66	0	Fiji

	P	W	D	L	PF	PA	Pts
South Africa	4	4	0	0	166	24	18
Wales	4	3	0	1	180	34	15
Samoa	4	2	0	2	91	49	10
Fiji	4	1	0	3	59	167	5
Namibia	4	0	0	4	44	266	0

Quarter-Finals

Ireland	10	22	Wales
England	12	19	France
South Africa	9	11	Australia
New Zealand	33	10	Argentina

23 October 2011, Eden Park, Auckland
New Zealand captain Richie McCaw lifts the Webb Ellis Cup.

Semi-Finals

Wales	8	9	France
Australia	6	20	New Zealand

Third place play-off

Wales	18	21	Australia

Final

France	7	8	New Zealand

24 September 2011, Eden Park, Auckland
New Zealand's Brad Thorn in action with France's Pascal Pape during a line-out.

25 September 2011, Eden Park, Auckland
Samoa in blue take on Fiji in a Pool D clash. Samoa won 27-7 and by finishing third in the group gained automatic qualification to the 2015 World Cup.

KooGa
RUGBY
WORLD CUP
2011
KooGa
RUGBY
WORLD CUP
2011
KooGa
KooGa

23 October 2011, Eden Park, Auckland
New Zealand perform the Haka before the final, as France look unintimidated.
A stern-faced Thierry Dusautoir stands in the middle.

RUGBY
WORLD CUP
2011

1 October 2011, Regional Stadium, Wellington
Tonga's Viliami Ma'afu goes to make a pass during his side's 19-14 victory over France in Pool A.

1 October 2011, Regional Stadium, Wellington
Tonga's players celebrate a sensational win against France, in one of the all-time great upsets.

RUGBY WORLD CUP 2011

8 October 2011, Eden Park, Auckland
France's Maxime Medard is tackled by England's Ben Youngs and Courtney Lawes in their quarter-final clash.

25 September 2011, Eden Park, Auckland
Samoa's George Stowers flies in for his team's second try in a 27-7 win against Fiji.

8 October 2011, Regional Stadium, Wellington
Wales's Jonathan Davies scores a try against Ireland as his side progresses to the semi-final to play France.

9 October 2011, Eden Park, Auckland
New Zealand take on Argentina for a place in the semi-final. The All Blacks cruised to a 33-10 victory.

23 October 2011, Eden Park, Auckland
A dejected Thierry Dusautoir walks past the Webb Ellis Cup, after losing the final 8-7 to hosts New Zealand. The match remains the lowest-scoring World Cup Final.

15 October 2011, Eden Park, Auckland
A crucial moment in the first half of the semi-final between Wales and France. Welsh captain Sam Warburton is sent off after an illegal tackle on France's Vincent Clerc. Wales lost out by the smallest of margins and were denied a first ever appearance in the final, as the French came out 9-8 winners, to claim a place in their third final.

NZ

RUGBY
CUP
THE
IN UNION
TACKLE

16 October 2011, Eden Park, Auckland
Australia and New Zealand battle for possession in a line-out during the semi-final. The All Blacks came out on top 20-6.

2015
England and Wales

10 October 2015, Twickenham Stadium, London
Australia and Wales compete for possession in a line-out during their Pool A tie, in which the Wallabies came out 15-6 winners. Both teams had by this point already qualified for the quarter-final, at the expense of the hosts England.

2015: England and Wales

97 **Nicolás Sánchez of Argentina was the tournament's top points scorer**

Going into 2015, New Zealand, Australia and South Africa all had two World Cup titles each, although New Zealand's triumphs had been in home tournaments with both their winning finals played at Eden Park. A victory in 2015 would be the first on foreign soil and the one and only time that a team has successfully defended their world championship. For the first time there were no World Cup debutants, and the only change from 2011 was the presence of Uruguay instead of Russia. In general, it was a rugby tournament held in English football stadiums. Due to high ticket demands, rugby grounds (apart from the national stadiums such as Twickenham and Cardiff) were deemed too small to host matches and the majority of the games would take place at Premier League football grounds. Sandy Park (capacity 12,500) in Exeter and Kingsholm Stadium (capacity 16,500) in Gloucester would be the only club rugby stadiums to be used as venues.

The previous time England had been the primary host nation, in 1991, they got to the final. This time, however, they had their worst ever tournament and for the first time were knocked out in the group stages. Pool A was the 'group of death', with England, Wales and Australia fighting for the two qualifying places even though all three teams were ranked in the world's top four, in contrast with Pool C, where the second-highest-ranked team was Argentina. Wales coach Warren Gatland was critical of the draw, as it had been made three years earlier when the rankings were different, 'That's just ridiculous as far as I'm concerned. If they had followed the football model then we wouldn't be in this position.' Despite England having a ten-point lead against Wales at Twickenham, the Dragons made a comeback and with six minutes left on the clock they took a 28-25 lead. In the closing minutes England were awarded a penalty which would have drawn them level. Instead they went for the win, but lost possession and the game was over. In hindsight it was the wrong decision, as the draw would have seen England qualify ahead of Wales. A 33-13 defeat to Australia was the final nail in England's coffin and for the first time in World Cup history, the host nation was eliminated before the knockout stages.

8 **Julien Savea of New Zealand was the tournament's top try scorer**

The game of the tournament was Japan vs South Africa in Pool B in Brighton. With the Springboks 32-29 ahead and the clock approaching 80 minutes, Japan had possession of an attacking scrum five yards from the goal line. During mounting pressure, the Japanese were awarded a penalty to level the game, but they went for the win and the gamble paid off with a try in the 84th minute by Karne Hesketh as the Brighton crowd went wild. It was the biggest upset in World Cup history; however, Japan were still eliminated in the group stage while South Africa finished top and would advance to the semi-final.

In the quarter-finals, the All Blacks had registered their statement win of the tournament with a masterclass against the French. Four years earlier, the final between New Zealand and France was a tighter affair than expected, with the All Blacks winning by a single point, but in 2015 Les Bleus were annihilated 62-13 in Cardiff in one of the most one-sided games in World Cup history between two elite nations. With Australia seeing off Argentina in the semi-final it set up the first all-Oceania Rugby World Cup Final, the All Blacks having edged past South Africa 20-18 in the last four. The two countries had met three times before in World Cup history, with Australia 2-1 ahead overall. Before the kick-off, the Red Arrows flew over Twickenham and the sense of occasion was huge, with the winner being the first nation to win three world titles. New Zealand built up a 21-3 lead early into the second half with the highlight being an incredible solo try from Ma'a Nonu. The game was already looking over but Australia mounted a fightback and brought the margin to just four points with 16 minutes still remaining. Instead of folding under pressure, New Zealand then ran away with the final and scored 13 unanswered points to create history and win a hat-trick of World Cups. The match also created history with the highest amount of tries scored in a final, the teams combining for five as New Zealand went over three times and Australia scored two.

Pool A

England	35	11	Fiji
Wales	54	9	Uruguay
Australia	28	13	Fiji
England	25	28	Wales
Australia	65	3	Uruguay
Wales	23	13	Fiji
England	13	33	Australia
Fiji	47	15	Uruguay
Australia	15	6	Wales
England	60	3	Uruguay

	P	W	D	L	PF	PA	Pts
Australia	4	4	0	0	141	35	17
Wales	4	3	0	1	111	62	13
England	4	2	0	2	133	75	11
Fiji	4	1	0	3	84	101	5
Uruguay	4	0	0	4	30	226	0

Pool B

South Africa	32	34	Japan
Samoa	25	16	USA
Scotland	45	10	Japan
South Africa	46	6	Samoa
Scotland	39	16	USA
Samoa	5	26	Japan
South Africa	34	16	Scotland
South Africa	64	0	USA
Samoa	33	36	Scotland
USA	18	28	Japan

	P	W	D	L	PF	PA	Pts
South Africa	4	3	0	1	176	56	16
Scotland	4	3	0	1	136	93	14
Japan	4	3	0	1	98	100	12
Samoa	4	1	0	3	69	124	6
USA	4	0	0	4	50	156	0

Pool C

Tonga	10	17	Georgia
New Zealand	26	16	Argentina
New Zealand	58	14	Namibia
Argentina	54	9	Georgia
Tonga	35	21	Namibia
New Zealand	43	10	Georgia
Argentina	45	16	Tonga
Namibia	16	17	Georgia
New Zealand	47	9	Tonga
Argentina	64	19	Namibia

	P	W	D	L	PF	PA	Pts
New Zealand	4	4	0	0	174	49	19
Argentina	4	3	0	1	179	70	15
Georgia	4	2	0	2	53	123	8
Tonga	4	1	0	3	70	130	6
Namibia	4	0	0	4	70	174	1

Pool D

Ireland	50	7	Canada
France	32	10	Italy
France	38	11	Romania
Italy	23	18	Canada
Ireland	44	10	Romania
France	41	18	Canada
Ireland	16	9	Italy
Canada	15	17	Romania
Italy	32	22	Romania
France	9	24	Ireland

	P	W	D	L	PF	PA	Pts
Ireland	4	4	0	0	134	35	18
France	4	3	0	1	120	63	14
Italy	4	2	0	2	74	88	10
Romania	4	1	0	3	60	129	4
Canada	4	0	0	4	58	131	2

Quarter-Finals

South Africa	23	19	Wales
New Zealand	62	13	France
Ireland	20	43	**Argentina**
Australia	35	34	Scotland

31 October 2015, Twickenham Stadium, London
New Zealand celebrate after beating Australia in the final, and in doing so becoming the first ever nation to win two World Cups in a row.

Semi-Finals

South Africa	18	20	**New Zealand**
Argentina	15	29	**Australia**

Third place play-off

South Africa	24	13	Argentina

Final

New Zealand	34	17	Australia

18

19 September 2015, American Express Community Stadium, Brighton
Japan's Karne Hesketh scores a try in the last play of the game against South Africa in one of the great upsets in World Cup history, as the Japanese win 34-32.

31 October 2015, Twickenham Stadium, London
New Zealand perform the Haka before the final against Australia.

10

RUGBY WORLD CUP 2015
IRFU
canterbury

18 October 2015, Millennium Stadium, Cardiff
Ireland's Luke Fitzgerald in action during the quarter-final match with Argentina.

Argentina's Juan Imhoff scores a try against Ireland, helping his team to reach the semi-final with a 43-20 victory.

17 October 2015, Millennium Stadium, Cardiff
New Zealand's Jerome Kaino scores a try in the quarter-final clash with France to help the All Blacks to a comprehensive 62-13 victory and set up a semi-final against South Africa.

31 October 2015, Twickenham Stadium, London
New Zealand's Ma'a Nonu runs past the Australian defence to score his team's second try in the final.

25 October 2015, Twickenham Stadium, London
Australia defeat Argentina by 29-15 in the semi-final. The South Americans would not repeat their bronze medal success of 2007, and would lose to South Africa in the bronze medal match five days later.

24 October 2015, Twickenham Stadium, London
New Zealand's prolific kicker Dan Carter scores a penalty against South Africa in which the All Blacks won 20-18 to progress to the final.

31 October 2015, Twickenham Stadium, London
The home of rugby is ready for the first ever all Oceania Rugby World Cup Final, as New Zealand take on Australia.

RUGBY WORLD CUP 2015
England 2015
#RWC2015
THE WORLD IN UNION

MEDIC
APAN日本2019

13 October 2019, International Stadium, Yokohama
Japan celebrate beating Scotland 28-21 and topping Pool A.

2019
Japan

2019: Japan

69 **Handré Pollard of South Africa scored the most points**

The choice of the host nation for 2019 marked a wholesale change of approach from the IRB, in that all previous World Cups had been played in a country that was a rugby powerhouse, and one of the sport's elite nations. 2019 marked the first time the World Cup had gone somewhere where rugby is very much a minority game, to the point where it's not even in the top ten most popular sports in the country. But that didn't stop good attendance figures throughout the tournament, with the notable exception of three games which had to be cancelled because of Typhoon Hagibis. England vs France, New Zealand vs Italy, and Namibia vs Canada were all pool games declared 0-0 draws due to the cancellations.

Japan could not have wished for a better outcome in the pool stages. Despite being ranked as the 11th overall seed they won their group with a 100 per cent record and beat both Scotland and Ireland. Against Ireland the hosts had to come back from a 12-3 deficit to win the game, and the victory against Scotland was a classic; the 'Brave Blossoms' took a 28-7 lead early into the second half and the game already looked over, before 'Scotland the Brave' scored two converted tries in just five minutes to take it to a one-possession game and there was still 25 minutes left on the clock. Scotland threw everything at the Japanese in the closing stages but the hosts managed to survive the onslaught and the match ended 28-21. There would be no swashbuckling adventures for the hosts in the knockout stages, however, and South Africa would beat them comfortably in the quarter-finals 26-3, avenging the humiliating defeat Japan had inflicted on them in 2015.

The Springboks were seeded seventh before the tournament, and after losing to New Zealand in the opening game, it confirmed that the All Blacks looked very likely to complete three World Cup triumphs in a row. They cruised through the quarter-final 46-14 against Ireland, scoring seven tries along the way, and this set up a semi-final against England who had thrashed Australia 40-16. At the time, the opinion was that England and New Zealand were the top two teams in the world and that the winner of the semi-final would go on to be the world champions. England's response to the Haka would become famous and they formed a V shape as a challenge and looked totally unfazed as the defending champions carried out their iconic intimidation ritual. England were fined by the IRB as they had crossed the halfway line, despite the consensus that the All Blacks respect a challenge to the Haka and don't have a problem with it.

7 **Josh Adams of Wales was the tournament's top try scorer**

Despite a 9am GMT kick-off time, the World Cup Final would be the most-watched broadcast in the UK during 2019, with over 12 million viewers tuning in. Twelve years earlier, when England had faced South Africa in the 2007 final, they had entered the game as underdogs and pushed the Springboks all the way in a close game. This time England entered as favourites and were taken apart in a one-sided beatdown in which South Africa dominated the scrum.

A tipping point came in the opening minutes as tighthead prop Kyle Sinckler went in for a tackle and collided with team-mate Maro Itoje. Sinckler sustained a head injury and was substituted, meaning England would be weaker in the scrum against a powerful opponent. England couldn't sustain any rhythm, they were frustrated and beaten down, and throughout the game South African pressure forced them to concede eight penalties. Despite South Africa's dominance, with the score at 18-12 England were only one possession away from taking the lead, but then in the 66th minute Makazole Mapimpi became the first Springboks player to score a try in a World Cup Final, as both of South Africa's previous victories had been achieved via kicking points only. A second try followed from Cheslin Kolbe in the 77th minute and the game was over. South Africa became the first winner of the Rugby World Cup to have lost a game in the same tournament, and they equalled New Zealand's record of three overall victories, despite having played two fewer tournaments due to still being banned in 1987 and 1991.

Pool A

Japan	30	10	Russia
Ireland	27	3	Scotland
Russia	9	34	Samoa
Japan	19	12	Ireland
Scotland	34	0	Samoa
Ireland	35	0	Russia
Japan	38	19	Samoa
Scotland	61	0	Russia
Ireland	47	5	Samoa
Japan	28	21	Scotland

	P	W	D	L	PF	PA	Pts
Japan	4	4	0	0	115	62	19
Ireland	4	3	0	1	121	27	16
Scotland	4	2	0	2	119	55	11
Samoa	4	1	0	3	58	128	5
Russia	4	0	0	4	19	160	0

Pool B

New Zealand	23	13	South Africa
Italy	47	22	Namibia
Italy	48	7	Canada
South Africa	57	3	Namibia
New Zealand	63	0	Canada
South Africa	49	3	Italy
New Zealand	71	9	Namibia
South Africa	66	7	Canada
New Zealand	0	0	Italy
Namibia	0	0	Canada

	P	W	D	L	PF	PA	Pts
New Zealand	4	3	1	0	157	22	16
South Africa	4	3	0	1	185	36	15
Italy	4	2	1	1	98	78	12
Namibia	4	0	1	3	34	175	2
Canada	4	0	1	3	14	177	2

Pool C

France	23	21	Argentina
England	35	3	Tonga
England	45	7	USA
Argentina	28	12	Tonga
France	33	9	USA
England	39	10	Argentina
France	23	21	Tonga
Argentina	47	17	USA
England	0	0	France
USA	19	31	Tonga

	P	W	D	L	PF	PA	Pts
England	4	3	1	0	119	20	17
France	4	3	1	0	79	51	15
Argentina	4	2	0	2	106	91	11
Tonga	4	1	0	3	67	105	6
USA	4	0	0	4	52	156	0

Pool D

Australia	39	21	Fiji
Wales	43	14	Georgia
Fiji	27	30	Uruguay
Georgia	33	7	Uruguay
Australia	25	29	Wales
Georgia	10	45	Fiji
Australia	45	10	Uruguay
Wales	29	17	Fiji
Australia	27	8	Georgia
Wales	35	13	Uruguay

	P	W	D	L	PF	PA	Pts
Wales	4	4	0	0	136	69	19
Australia	4	3	0	1	136	68	16
Fiji	4	1	0	3	110	108	7
Georgia	4	1	0	3	65	122	5
Uruguay	4	1	0	3	60	140	4

Quarter-Finals

England	40	16	Australia
New Zealand	46	14	Ireland
Wales	20	19	France
Japan	3	26	South Africa

2 November 2019, International Stadium, Yokohama
South Africa defeat England 32-12 in the final and lift the Webb Ellis Cup for a record-equalling third time.

Semi-Finals

England	19	7	New Zealand
Wales	16	19	South Africa

Third place play-off

New Zealand	40	17	Wales

Final

England	12	32	South Africa

2 November 2019, International Stadium, Yokohama
Handre Pollard of South Africa in action against England in the final.

ENGLAND
ENGLAND

26 October 2019, International Stadium, Yokohama
England challenge the Haka before the semi-final. The team formed a V shape and were supposed to have moved further forward, but were too disorganised to do so! However, once the game started England put on an outstanding performance and won 19-7, to reach their fourth final.

24 September 2019, Kumagaya Rugby Stadium, Kumagaya
Samoa's Afaesetiti Amosa scores their second try against Russia in a Pool A match which the Samoans won 34-9.

WORLD CUP
埼玉県・

13 October 2019, Hanazono Rugby Stadium, Osaka
Tonga's Zane Kapeli in action with Ruben De Haas and Marcel Brache of the USA in a Pool C match which the southern hemisphere team won 31-19.

3 October 2019, Hanazono Rugby Stadium, Osaka
Fiji's Tevita Cavubati in action against Georgia in their Pool D match which the Fijians won 45-10.

ISC

13 October 2019, International Stadium, Yokohama
Japan players and fans celebrate together after beating Scotland in a classic encounter.

N14
RUGBY
WORLD CUP
YOKOHAMA
JAPAN

19 October 2019, Oita Stadium, Oita
Australia's Kurtley Beale in action against England. The northern hemisphere team reached the semi-final with a rousing 40-16 victory.

19 October 2019, Oita Stadium, Oita
England's Anthony Watson celebrates with his team-mates after scoring his side's fourth try to help them into the semi-final where they would face New Zealand.

13 October 2019, International Stadium, Yokohama
Scotland's Jamie Ritchie and Japan's Yu Tamura grab hold of one another.

13 October 2019, International Stadium, Yokohama
Scotland players are devastated after losing to Japan and being eliminated in the pool stages. They had fought back against Japan and were a converted try away from levelling, but the hosts held firm to win the game.

27 October 2019, International Stadium, Yokohama
South Africa's Faf De Klerk looks unintimidated as he is grabbed by the much larger Jake Ball of Wales.

27 October 2019, International Stadium, Yokohama
In the same game, Faf De Klerk tries to take down Wales's Ross Moriarty. The South Africans won 19-16 to advance to the final.

26 October 2019, International Stadium, Yokohama
England rise above New Zealand during a line-out in their semi-final victory over the All Blacks, winning 19-7 to set up a final against South Africa.

England's Ben Youngs celebrates scoring a try with team-mates that is later disallowed after a TMO review. It didn't prevent England from reaching the final.

27 October 2019, International Stadium, Yokohama
Wales' Dan Biggar in action against South Africa but he couldn't help prevent the Springboks from reaching the final.

1987 NEW ZEALAND
1991 AUSTRALIA
1995 SOUTH AFRICA
1999 AUSTRALIA
2003 ENGLAND
2007 SOUTH AFRICA

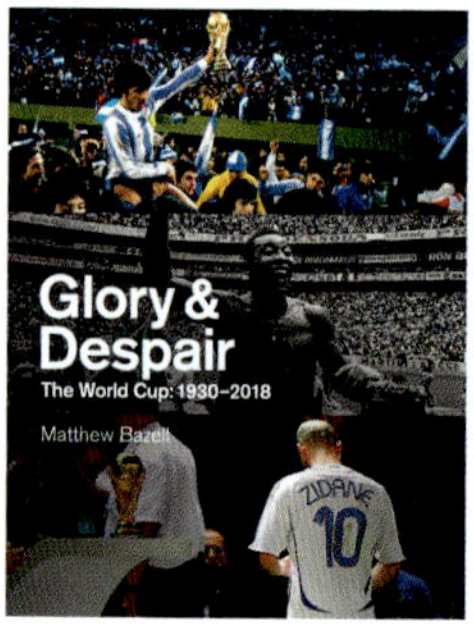

More from Matthew Bazell

I would like to thank everyone who has bought a copy of this book for supporting authors and print media. Thanks to my parents Catherine Bazell and Ben Bazell for proofreading duties. I would like to say thanks to Pitch Publishing for sharing the same vision of the book as I did, and for being easy to work with. I'd like to dedicate the book to my nieces the double V's....Veronica Bazell and Vivienne Delaney.